Adam
Frost

THE
AWESOME
BODY BOOK

The world's most
INCREDIBLE
human
body FACTS

BLOOMSBURY
N OXFORD NEW YORK NEW DELHI SYDNEY

To Anna and Eliza

Published 2016 by Bloomsbury Publishing Plc
50 Bedford Square, London, WC1B 3DP
www.bloomsbury.com
Bloomsbury is a registered trademark of Bloomsbury Publishing Plc

ISBN: 978-1-4088-6235-3

Produced for Bloomsbury Publishing Plc by Dutch&Dane

With thanks to Joseph Gwinn

A CIP record for this book is available from the British Library.

Printed in China by Leo Paper Products, Heshan, Guangdong

1 3 5 7 9 10 8 6 4 2

All figures used in this book are believed to be the latest and most accurate figures at
the point of publication, unless the copy states otherwise. Where figures are estimates
or approximations, we have tried to make this clear. A selection of books and websites
we used for our facts can be found on the Sources page at the back of the book.

YOUR BRILLIANT BODY

Even when you're reading this page, your body's hard at work.

Your heart is beating at around 70 beats per minute.

Your lungs are breathing about 10 times a minute.

Your stomach and intestines are digesting food – aided by about 100 trillion bacteria.

Your spine is keeping you upright.

Your mouth is producing saliva – up to 1 litre a day.

To help you read, your eye muscles are moving almost 200 times every minute.

...meanwhile, your bottom releases about 14 farts per day.

There are trillions of synapses firing in your brain.

So let's start the BODY COUNTDOWN...

THE AWESOME BODY COUNTDOWN

Ready for lift-off..?

10

10 per cent of all the world's people are left-handed.

9

The biggest human nose is almost 9cm long. It belongs to Mehmet Ozyurek.

8

Humans need about 8 hours of sleep a day. Giraffes need 2 hours, while koala bears need roughly 22 hours.

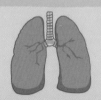

7

The average fart travels at about 7 miles per hour (11km/h).

6

People breathe an average of 6 litres of air every minute, when at rest.

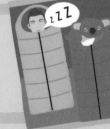

5

You have about 5 million hairs on your body. A chimpanzee has a similar amount, but more of your hairs are see-through.

4

4 per cent of people have a 'sticky-out' belly button.

3

You can survive for 3 minutes without breathing, 3 days without drinking and about 3 weeks without eating.

2

Your toenails grow at just under 2mm per month (your fingernails grow twice as fast).

1

You swallow about 1 litre of snot every day.

ZERO

And ZERO is... the number of people who can sneeze with their eyes open, tickle themselves or hum while holding their nose.

WHAT AM I?

I'm glad you asked.

YOU ARE... 7 OCTILLION ATOMS:

7,000,000,000, X 000,000,000,000, 000,000

A flea

There's a lot of space between them, though.

If you didn't have this space in-between your atoms, your entire body would fit into THIS BOX:

YOU ARE... more than 37 trillion (37,000,000,000,000) cells:

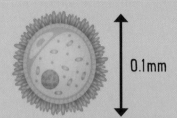

0.1mm

The largest cell in the human body (if you're female) is the egg cell or 'ovum'.

It's about 0.1mm wide. That's about the same width as a human hair.

The longest cells are in the 'sciatic' nerve that runs from your spinal cord to your big toe.

They can be up to 1 METRE long... ...but they are only about 0.000001m (1 micrometer) wide.

YOU ARE...
A MIXTURE OF CHEMICAL ELEMENTS:

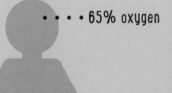

•••• 65% oxygen

•••• 19% carbon

•••• 10% hydrogen

•••• 6% other things

Like every plant and animal on Earth, you are a 'carbon-based' life form.

Without carbon, you'd just be a heap of random atoms.

Most of the oxygen in your body is found in water.

YOU ARE... BONES, MUSCLES, BLOOD AND MORE:

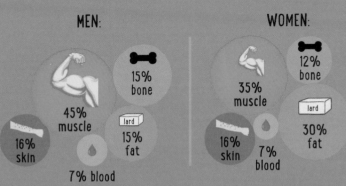

MEN:

15% bone

45% muscle

16% skin

lard 15% fat

7% blood

WOMEN:

12% bone

35% muscle

lard 30% fat

16% skin

7% blood

Women have more fat than men – this is because their bodies are designed to protect and insulate a growing baby.

HOW TO MAKE A POO
12:00–12:10pm
EAT FOOD

FEED ME!!

Your jaws and teeth tear and chew the food.

Your saliva breaks down chemicals in the food.

The jaw muscle is the strongest muscle in the human body.

150 Newtons is the bite force needed to chew most food.

700 Newtons is the MAXIMUM human bite force.

Zsolt Sinka pulled a 50-TONNE aeroplane over 39 METRES using just a rope and his teeth.

You make 1 litre of saliva a day. So...

In a year, you could fill...

Four bathtubs with your slimy SPIT.

12:10-4:00pm
DIGEST FOOD IN STOMACH

FOOD MAKES ITS WAY TO YOUR STOMACH IN ABOUT 5-10 SECONDS...

...powerful muscles churn the food. Strong acids dissolve the food.

An empty stomach can expand in volume from...

0.5 litres

to

3 litres

It can become almost as big as a football.*

*All these measurements are for adults' stomachs. Children's are a bit smaller.

Stomach acids can dissolve...

bone ✓

wood ✓

metal ✓

chewing gum ✓

...but please don't swallow ANY of these things!

Stomach acid would eat through your flesh if your stomach walls weren't coated with a yucky, acid-resistant MUCUS.

4:00pm-9:00pm
PUSH FOOD THROUGH YOUR SMALL INTESTINE

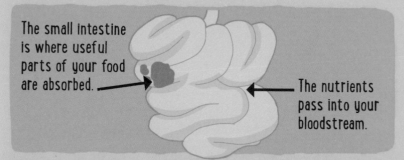

The small intestine is where useful parts of your food are absorbed.

The nutrients pass into your bloodstream.

Your small intestine is home to about **100 TRILLION** bacteria. (Most of them are helpful.)

The small intestine is not that small!

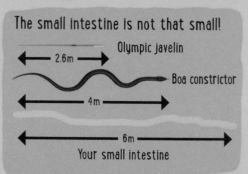

Olympic javelin — 2.6m

Boa constrictor — 4m

Your small intestine — 6m

Other mammals have even l o n g e r small intestines.

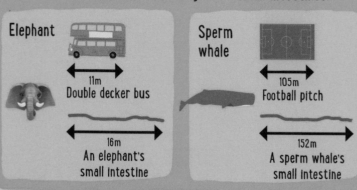

Elephant

Double decker bus — 11m

An elephant's small intestine — 16m

Sperm whale

Football pitch — 105m

A sperm whale's small intestine — 152m

9:00pm–1:00pm (16 hours in total)
SEND FOOD INTO YOUR LARGE INTESTINE

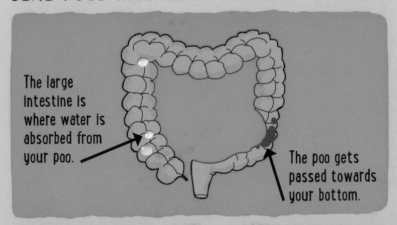

The large intestine is where water is absorbed from your poo.

The poo gets passed towards your bottom.

At this point, your poo is getting its colour and smell.

Colour: ...from waste iron and dead blood cells.

BROWN

Smell: ...from dead bacteria.

The large intestine is actually shorter than the small intestine...

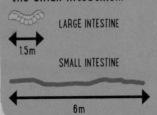

LARGE INTESTINE

1.5m

SMALL INTESTINE

6m

...but it's a lot wider...

It's about 30 per cent of the size of whatever you ate.

The small intestine is as wide as a 50p coin, while the large intestine is as wide as a tennis ball:

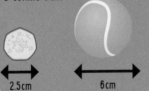

2.5cm

6cm

1:00pm: more than a day later...
...IT'S POO TIME!

BRISTOL STOOL CHART: A scale used by doctors to judge how healthy your poos are.

CONSTIPATION
(eat more fibre!)

1   Hard lumps, like nuts.

2   Like a lumpy sausage.

3   Like a sausage, but with cracks on the surface.

4   Like a (brown) snake, smooth and soft.

A HEALTHY POO

5   Squishy blobs.

6   Fluffy and mushy

7   Watery or completely liquid.

DIARRHOEA
(go to the doctor)

ANY QUESTIONS..?

Q1: How did the sweetcorn get in there?

Your stomach acid can melt razor blades. But yes, that sweetcorn has survived to make it into your poo... Well, sort of.

In fact, it's just the OUTER SHELLS. Your stomach can digest all the nutritious pulp inside the corn kernels, but doesn't have the right enzyme (a chemical) for breaking down their outer layers.

Q2: How do you poo in a spacesuit?

The simple answer is – you wear a giant nappy. However, if you're walking around on the Moon, you have the chance to leave your waste behind.

In other words, THERE'S POO ON THE MOON.

Q3: How long do OTHER animals take to make a poo?

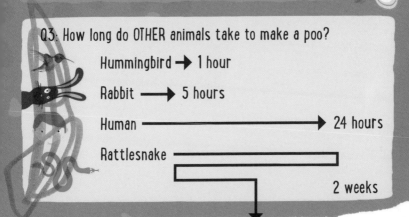

Hummingbird → 1 hour

Rabbit → 5 hours

Human → 24 hours

Rattlesnake

2 weeks

IN ONE END...
During an average lifetime, you'll eat about THIS much food:

30 tonnes
That's roughly the same weight as:

5 elephants

And you'll produce
THIS much poo:

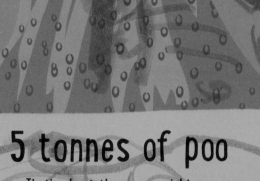

5 tonnes of poo

That's about the same weight as:

6 small cars

DIRTY GREAT DUNGHILLS

Other animals make our poo look puny. In a lifetime, each of the following animals produces...

 FLOWER POWER

Plant-eaters (also known as 'herbivores') tend to poo more because they eat more. Plants are harder to digest, so herbivores often eat large amounts to get all the nutrients they need.

A dog:
0.5 tonnes

A human:
5 tonnes

A horse:
200 tonnes

KING PONG!!

When meat-eaters poo, it tends to smell worse because meat protein has more sulphides in it. Fortunately, top poo-ers such as elephants and horses are plant-eaters. PHEW!!

A cow:
385 tonnes

An elephant:
1,095 tonnes

INCREDIBLE EDIBLES

Feeling peckish? Many of the things in your back garden or local park are edible...

Dandelions
The leaves are very tasty in a salad.

Clover
Small amounts are good for you – usually boiled or juiced to make the leaves easier to digest.

Stinging nettles
You can use them to make tea. Or you can add them to soup or pasta. Be careful when you pick them though..!

Dock leaves
You can rub these on your leg after a stinging nettle gets you. But most kinds of dock leaf are tasty, too.

Pass the grass

Okay, so you can't eat the green stuff on your lawn... you'd need four stomachs (like a cow has) to digest THAT type of grass. But did you know that wheat, oats, corn and rice are all types of grass? And they're delicious...

Roses

Rose petals are used in many kinds of dishes. The white base of the petal tends to be bitter, so chop that bit off.

Insects

People from many different cultures eat bugs. You can get centipedes on sticks in China, fried crickets in Mexico and boiled earthworms in Venezuela. Tuck in!

Daisies

The flowers may taste a little bitter, but the leaves are yummy additions to a salad.

NASTY NATURE

Nature has also given us some powerful poisons.
These are some of the deadliest...

Just 1 teaspoon of
each poison could kill:*

Venom of the Brazilian wandering spider...

 ...500 PEOPLE

Venom of the inland taipan (the world's deadliest snake)...

 ...JUST OVER 2,600 PEOPLE

Ricin (from the castor oil plant)...

 ...3,000 PEOPLE

Barachotoxin (from the poison dart frog)...

 ...ALMOST 25,000 PEOPLE

KEY
= 100
PEOPLE

*Assuming a teaspoon is about 5g of poison and the average adult
is 75kg in weight. In reality, it's all a lot more complicated...

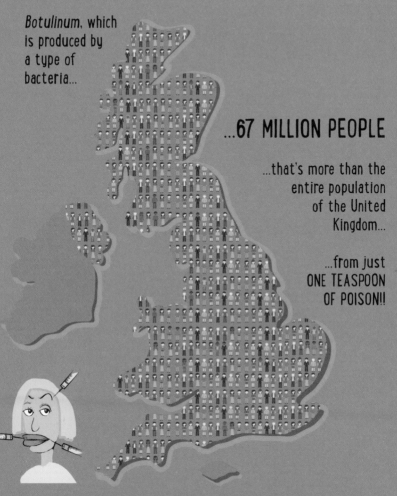

Botulinum, which
is produced by
a type of
bacteria...

...67 MILLION PEOPLE

...that's more than the
entire population
of the United
Kingdom...

...from just
ONE TEASPOON
OF POISON!!

As well as being the most deadly poison in the world, *botulinum*
is used to make 'botox' – a beauty product that some people
inject into their faces to smooth out their wrinkles!

Also: look
out for THESE
natural nasties...

RHUBARB LEAVES
Although purple rhubarb stems are edible, don't eat the leaves. They're poisonous!

YEW TREES
Most parts of a yew tree are poisonous. Eating just a few of its needles is enough to kill you.

FOXGLOVES
They're a common sight in fields and woodlands, but BEWARE... the whole plant is poisonous – and the leaves at the top are the deadliest.

OLEANDER
It's one of the most common garden plants in the world, and EVERY PART of it is poisonous. If you burn it, even the smoke is toxic!

DEATH CAP MUSHROOMS
A common sight in British forests, just 28g (1 ounce) is enough to kill a human. They've been used throughout history by monstrous murderers – and were probably used to poison the Roman Emperor Claudius.

BURN BABY BURN

So, you've just eaten a GIGANTIC meal. What's the best way to burn off those calories?

 **+** **=**  1,000 calories

A HUGE plate of spaghetti Bolognese

One BIG bowl of ice cream

RUN FOR 3½ hours

SWIM FOR 5 HOURS

DANCE FOR 5½ HOURS

ICE SKATE FOR 6 HOURS

WALK FOR ABOUT 9 HOURS

SPEND 13 HOURS TEN-PIN BOWLING

Of course, you're using up energy all the time – by talking, thinking, breathing, and so on – and you even burn calories while you're asleep...
...so you don't actually NEED to go bowling for 13 hours.

TALKING TOUGH

You have more than 600 muscles in your body and they come in a variety of shapes and sizes.

The smallest muscle...
is in your ear! Your *stapedius* is 1mm long and protects you from high noise levels.

The coolest muscles...
are also in your ear. The *auriculares* control outer ear movement and they're why 15 per cent of us can WIGGLE OUR EARS.

The strangest muscle...
is your tongue. Unlike every other muscle. it's only attached at one end. That's why you can stick it out!

The cleverest muscles...
are the muscles that work without us thinking about them.

The heart muscles: they keep our hearts beating through every moment of our lives.

The biggest muscle...
is in your bottom! Your *gluteus maximus* helps you to stand upright.

The longest muscle...
is in your leg. Your *sartorius* goes from your hip to the back of your knee. If you've ever looked at the bottom of your shoe to check for dog poo, you've used it.

The muscles around our iris: they automatically decide how much light to let into our eyes.

The muscles in our digestive system: they contract to pass food through our bodies.

FULL BODY WORKOUT

How many of your muscles do you use for different tasks?

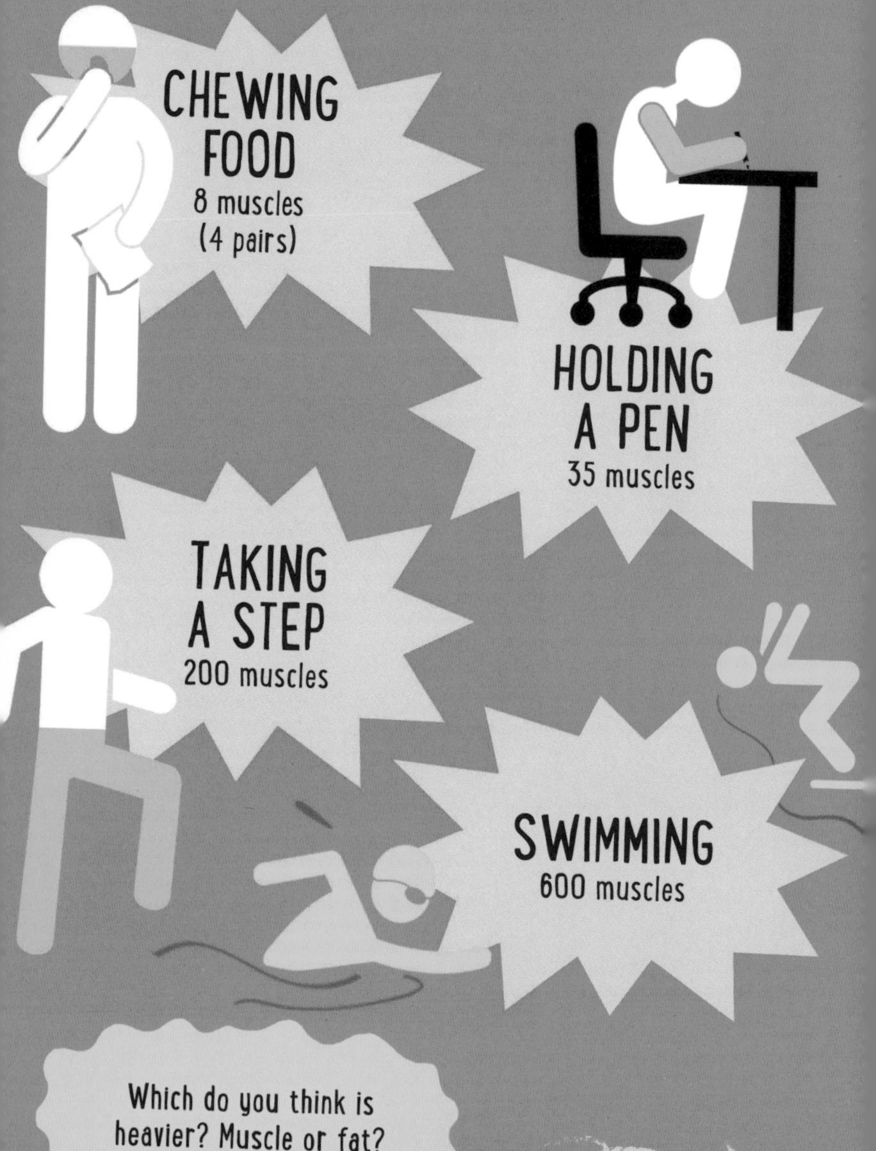

CHEWING FOOD
8 muscles
(4 pairs)

HOLDING A PEN
35 muscles

TAKING A STEP
200 muscles

SWIMMING
600 muscles

Which do you think is heavier? Muscle or fat?

SUPERHUMAN

Some people have done some AMAZING things with their muscles.

British man John Evans has balanced a car on his head! He kept the 159kg Mini on his head for 33 seconds, WITHOUT using his hands.

Victorian giant Angus MacAskill (1825-63) lifted a fully-grown horse over a 1.2-metre-high fence.

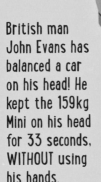

US strongman Joe Rollino once lifted 288kg (about the same weight as a grand piano) using just ONE FINGER.

Alain Robert has climbed the Eiffel Tower in Paris, France, without any safety equipment or climbing gear. All he used were his climbing shoes and the muscles in his arms and legs.

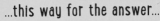
...this way for the answer...

FACE TIME

The muscles in your face can pull over 7,000 different expressions. The most common are these six (below).

ANGER
Your big brother won't give back the comic he borrowed.

FEAR
You heard something go BUMP in the night.

DISGUST
Brussels sprouts! YUCK!!

SURPRISE
Your best friend just did a double backflip.

JOY
It's the school holidays!

SADNESS
You got left out of the school football team (again).

ANSWER
MUSCLE! Muscle tissue is more dense than fat. So if you do a lot of exercise and make your muscles bigger, then sometimes your weight can go up!

However... Scientists have also identified 15 others.
Here are eight of them:

AWED
You're at a fireworks display.

HATRED
Your face when someone is being SERIOUSLY mean.

APPALLED
Your mum when she realises you ate ten bags of crisps.

HAPPILY DISGUSTED
Your friend has just shown you an AWESOME scab.

ANGRILY DISGUSTED
Your sister left her dirty socks on your bed.

SADLY ANGRY
You just got sent to bed early.

HAPPILY SURPRISED
Your sister at her surprise birthday party.

FEARFULLY DISGUSTED
Your little brother is about to wipe snot on you.

The other seven are: sadly fearful, sadly surprised, sadly disgusted, fearfully angry, fearfully surprised, angrily surprised and disgustedly surprised.

EXPRESS YOURSELF: How many of these faces can you pull?

HAPPY TALK

Some people say, *"Cheer up! It takes more muscles to frown than to smile..!"* But most scientists think smiling is harder work.

SMALL FROWN:	SLIGHT SMILE:	NORMAL FROWN:	NORMAL SMILE:
6 muscles	10 muscles	11 muscles	12 muscles

CAN YOU RECOGNISE A *FAKE* SMILE..?

In a FAKE smile, only the *zygomatic major* muscle (running from the cheekbone to the corner of the lips) is being used.

In a REAL smile, the *orbicularis oculi (pars lateralis)* is being used. This means the eyelids may fold and the ends of the eyebrows may dip slightly.

In other words, a FAKE smile never reaches the eyes!

CHEESE!

In the UK, we say *"Cheese!"* when we need to smile for the camera. But what do they say in other countries?

DENMARK

APPELSIN! (ORANGE)

SPAIN

PATATA! (POTATO)

RUSSIA

IZYUM! (RAISINS)

CHINA

QIÉZI! (AUBERGINE)

INDONESIA

BUNCIS! (GREEN BEANS)

FRANCE

OUISTITI (MARMOSET)

THE TREMENDOUS TONGUE

The tongue really is a multi-talented muscle. Here are some of the things it does:

Prepares food for chewing.

Lets you know what your food tastes like.

Helps you to speak.

Helps you to swallow.

Helps to keep your teeth clean in-between brushing.

Can be stuck out at people who annoy you.

Filters out nasty germs (via cells in the lingual tonsils).

Your tongue has around 10,000 taste buds on it. It can detect five different types of tastes.

SALTY Crisps NUTS Salt CHIPS

SOUR Lemons Kiwi fruit Grapes Vinegar

BITTER coffee DARK chocolate Olives Chicory

SWEET sugar Bananas honey Carrots

SAVOURY soy sauce Ham Cheese Potatoes

TRY THIS Dry your tongue with a paper towel. Then balance a sugar cube on it. Taste anything? Without saliva, it is very difficult to taste your food.

Is it possible to SWALLOW your tongue?

HUMAN V ANIMAL

Do we have more taste buds than other animals?

THE NUMBER OF TASTE BUDS IN HUMANS AND OTHER ANIMALS:

| SONGBIRDS: 50 | PARROTS: 350 | LIONS: 450 | DOGS: 1,700 |

| HUMAN ADULT (50yrs): 5,000 | HUMAN CHILD (8yrs): 10,000 | RABBITS: 17,000 | COWS: 25,000 |

 Plant-eating animals (such as cows and rabbits) need more taste buds because they help them to identify plants that might be poisonous.

No!

It's tied to the bottom of your mouth by a frenulum.

Catfish have 250,000 taste buds – all over their bodies! This helps them to detect food particles in the water as they swim through it.

When it comes to tongue length, other animals definitely have us licked...

The average human tongue: 10 centimetres

Aardvark tongue: 30 centimetres

An aardvark's tongue is long, sticky and worm-like. This helps it to hoover up termites in their long, curvy nests.

Giraffe tongue: 50 centimetres

The blue whale's tongue weighs as much as an elephant. As many as 50 people could stand on it, with room to spare!

Anteater tongue: 60 centimetres

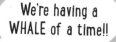

We're having a WHALE of a time!!

Blue whale tongue: 6-7 metres

If we measured animal tongues in comparison to body length, humans would be even further behind...

That'tth ttho ttthort!!

HUMAN BEING: 0.06 x BODY LENGTH

Average body length: 175cm
Tongue length: 10cm

LUNGLESS SALAMANDER: 0.8 x BODY LENGTH

Average body length: 6.5cm
Tongue length: 5cm

CHAMELEON: 1 x BODY LENGTH

Average body length: 70cm
Tongue length: 70cm

TUBE-LIPPED NECTAR BAT: 1.5 x BODY LENGTH

Average body length: 5.5cm
Tongue length: 8.5cm

AFRICAN HAWKMOTH: 3 x BODY LENGTH

Average body length: 7cm
Tongue length: 20cm

The hawkmoth's tongue has EVOLVED to be as long as it is. It allows the moth to reach the nectar at the bottom of a Madagascan orchid (right).

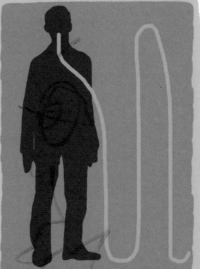

The salamander has the fastest tongue – it shoots out and back again in just 20 milliseconds (that's 20 *thousandths* of a second).

If your tongue was as long as an African hawkmoth's, when compared to your overall body size, it would look a bit like this.

I've got my eye on that fly!

Who NEEDS a tongue?
The northern leopard frog uses its EYES to help it swallow. After putting an insect in its mouth, it pushes its eyeballs back into its body, forcing the insect down its throat.

True or False?
Your tongue print is as unique as your fingerprints.

LET'S TWIST AGAIN

Some sentences are hard to wrap your tongue around.

Try saying each of these 10 times in a row – as FAST as you can.

Red lorry yellow lorry red lorry yellow lorry.
Round the rugged rock the ragged rascal ran.

Or how about this one?

She sells sea-shells on the sea-shore.
The shells she sells are sea-shells, I'm sure.
For if she sells sea-shells on the sea-shore
Then I'm sure she sells sea-shore shells.

But... THIS one is 'officially' the toughest:

The sixth sick sheikh's sixth sheep's sick

True!
The shape and texture of your tongue are completely unique.

EWWW!!

Some kids pick up nasty habits...

27%
of children bite
their fingernails.

10%
bite their
toenails.

43%
of kids pick
their scabs.

But grown-ups can be even **worse**...

20%
of adults don't wash
their hands after
going to the toilet.

20%
say they wee in
the pool when they
go swimming.

22%
aren't even
wearing clean
underwear...

So... Grown-ups are definitely **GROSSER** than kids..!

THE FACTS ABOUT FARTS

Breaking news about breaking wind...

The average number of
farts per person per day **=** **14**

Men and women fart
about the same amount.

AVERAGE SPEEDS (in kilometres per hour)

A HUMAN (WALKING):
5km/h

A FART:
11km/h

A SNEEZE:
63km/h

If you captured the farts of everyone
in Britain IN A SINGLE DAY, you could fill:

11 HOT AIR BALLOONS*

*Based on an average, four-person hot air balloon
containing roughly 2,800 cubic metres of gas.

We breathe in about a litre of OTHER PEOPLE'S FARTS every day.

Here are the foods that produce...

The MOST farts:

 Beans

 Fruits

 Fizzy drinks

The SMELLIEST farts:

 Eggs

 Meat

 Broccoli

Eggs and meat contain the most sulphur, which is the part of your fart that provides the smell.

SULPHUR: Only 1 per cent of your farts are sulphur. The other 99 per cent are made up of gases such as nitrogen and carbon dioxide, which don't smell at all.

ANY QUESTIONS?

THE BIG QUESTIONS

You OK?!

Q: IF YOU HOLD A FART IN, WILL IT GO AWAY?

A: **NO.** There's only one way out. Although it sometimes feels like a fart has 'disappeared', it usually leaks out slowly or comes back later.

Q: DO LOUD FARTS SMELL LESS?

A: **YES.** Many farts are produced by swallowing air when you eat or breathe. Air contains mostly odourless gases. These tend to produce larger, louder air bubbles. So... when you release them, they may be louder – but they won't be as lethal.

Silent farts, on the other hand, tend to be small and full of sulphur. They truly are 'silent but deadly'.

Q: CAN YOU TEACH YOURSELF TO FART WHENEVER YOU LIKE?

Oink!

A: **NO.** At least, MOST people can't. But now and again you get someone like Joseph Pujol (1857–1945), the French 'fartiste'. He could fart songs, play musical instruments with his bottom and even imitate farmyard animals with his incredible farts.

Q: CAN YOU SET LIGHT TO YOUR OWN FARTS?

A: **YES.** Farts contain flammable gases such as methane and hydrogen. Depending on the make-up of your fart, the flame produced will be:

 BLUE (if it contains methane)*

ORANGE (if it contains hydrogen)

*Only about half of the population have methane in their farts.

SAFETY INFORMATION: fart-lighting is **INCREDIBLY** dangerous and can lead to incidents like this...

📣 DAILY BUGLE

UP IN SMOKE

In 2012, a 12-year-old boy from Tipton, in England, decided to hold a fart-lighting competition with his cousin.

He accidentally set light to a nearby petrol can – which blew up. The boy was taken to hospital with serious injuries on the backs of his legs.

The fire fighter who rescued him said, "I think he must have won the competition but he will have some nasty burns now. It is a warning not to mess around with fire."

FOREIGN BODIES

Think you're alone? Think again. Your body is a 'microbiome' – full of tiny little lives.

BACTERIA

90 per cent of the cells in your body aren't even yours.

Your body has:

About 37 trillion
(37,000,000,000,000)
body cells.

More than 300 trillion
(300,000,000,000,000)
bacteria cells.

MITES

About half of all adults
have mites in their
eyebrows.

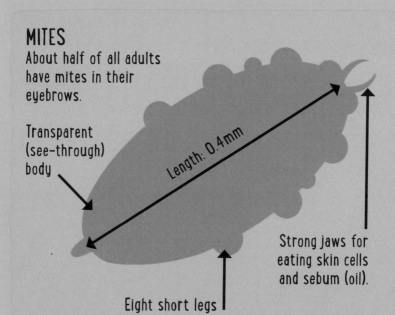

Transparent
(see-through)
body

Length: 0.4mm

Strong jaws for
eating skin cells
and sebum (oil).

Eight short legs

WORMS

For most of history, human beings have hosted worms in their stomachs and intestines.

PINWORMS
The most common type of worm.

About 30 per cent of the world's children have them, and it is more common in less developed countries.

TAPEWORMS
Tapeworms can live happily for years in your bowels without you even noticing. As a result, they can get SERIOUSLY long.

Longest known python: 7.7m

The longest tapeworm ever recorded: 33m.

OTHER BUGS

Sometimes, other creepy crawlies can hitch a ride.

 Danielle Eccles from Halstead, UK, had a ladybird in her ear for three years.

 PK Krishnamurthy of Mumbai, India, had a 12.5-centimetre worm removed from his eye.

 Doctors in Cambridge, UK, found a tapeworm that had been living in a man's brain for four years.

 Changsea hospital in China found a spider living in a woman's ear.

 Twelve-year-old Anil Barela – of Madhya Pradesh, in India – had to have a live fish removed from his lung after accidentally inhaling it when playing in a river.

BRILLIANT BONES

Think skeletons are spooky? Well, there's one inside you right now!

Your skull starts out as seven separate plates of bone that can move about. This is because a baby's head needs to fit through its mother's narrow birth canal. By the age of two, these plates have fused (joined) together.

When you were a baby, you had more than 300 bones and cartilage elements. As you grew up, lots of these gradually fused together – leaving you with 206.

Your teeth are considered to be part of your skeleton, but they are NOT counted as bones. Bones contain periosteum, which means they can mend themselves if they get broken. Your teeth cannot do this!

Your funny bone isn't actually a bone. It's your ulnar nerve, which is why it hurts when you knock it. Not very 'funny' at all!

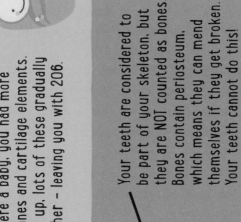

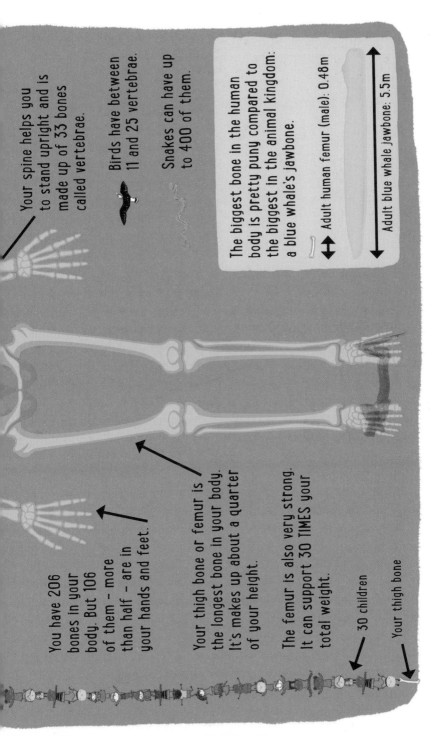

Your spine helps you to stand upright and is made up of 33 bones called vertebrae.

Birds have between 11 and 25 vertebrae.

Snakes can have up to 400 of them.

The biggest bone in the human body is pretty puny compared to the biggest in the animal kingdom: a blue whale's jawbone.

Adult human femur (male): 0.48m

Adult blue whale jawbone: 5.5m

You have 206 bones in your body. But 106 of them – more than half – are in your hands and feet.

Your thigh bone or femur is the longest bone in your body. It's makes up about a quarter of your height.

The femur is also very strong. It can support 30 TIMES your total weight.

30 children

Your thigh bone

SNAP!

Evil Kneivel, a motorcycle stuntman, holds the world record for the most broken bones. Here are just SOME of the bones he smashed during his career.

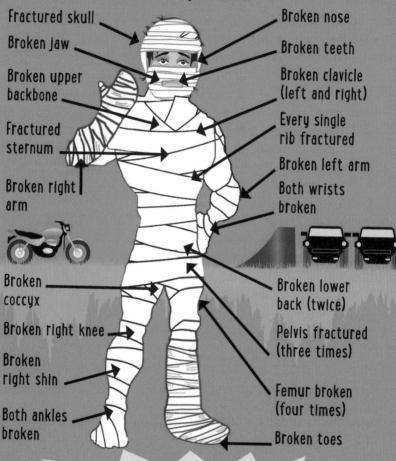

Fractured skull

Broken jaw

Broken upper backbone

Fractured sternum

Broken right arm

Broken coccyx

Broken right knee

Broken right shin

Both ankles broken

Broken nose

Broken teeth

Broken clavicle (left and right)

Every single rib fractured

Broken left arm

Both wrists broken

Broken lower back (twice)

Pelvis fractured (three times)

Femur broken (four times)

Broken toes

Number of times he broke one of his bones:
433

JOIN US!

All of your bones (except one*) are connected to other bones by joints. Some joints are more mobile than others.

Don't move →

Synarthrosis joint — Examples include the joints that connect your teeth to your skull.

Gliding joint — Some of the bones in your wrist move by gliding against their neighbouring bones.

Hinge joint — These joints include your knee and your elbow. They move like the hinges of a door.

Move a bit

Pivot joint — The pivot joint in your neck lets you turn your head around.

Saddle joint — These exist only in your thumbs. They can move back and forth and side to side. They also rotate (a bit).

Move a lot — Ball and socket joint — Examples include your hips and your shoulders. These incredible joints allow you to move your arms and legs in multiple directions.

QUESTION: How many bones does a shark have?

*(The hyoid bone in your neck.)

HAIR TO SPARE

Here are some hair-raising facts about your hair.

You have about 5 million hairs on your body.

Around 100,000 of them are on your head (unless you're bald).

Only a few parts of your body have NO HAIR AT ALL.

These include:

 i) Your lips

 ii) The palms of your hands

 iii) The soles of your feet

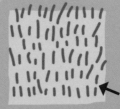

On each square inch of your skin, there are about 65 hairs.

Count them!

Each hair has its own blood, muscle and nerve supply. This allows each individual hair to...

...grow.   ...stick up when it's cold.   ...feel when something touches it.

None. A shark's skeleton is made up of cartilage, which is lighter and more flexible than bone. The end of your nose is built out of cartilage, too.

The hair on your head grows about 1cm each month.

| 1 | 2 | 3 | 4 | 5 | 6 | 7 | 8 | 9 | 10 | 11 | 12 |

centimetres (cm)

Scale = actual size

Six months to get this long...   ...a year to get this long.

Kazuhiro Watanabe, a fashion designer from Japan, has the world's tallest 'Mohawk' hairstyle. It took him a full 15 years to grow it.

1.1m

Indian grocer Radhakant Baijpai has ear hair measuring 25cm, which is a world record.

25cm

The longest leg hair belongs to Guido Arturo of Italy. It measures just over 19cm.

Camarasaurus was 18m in length

16.8-m-long braided hair

Asha Mandela has 16.8-metre-long dreadlocks. They weigh about 20kg – almost as heavy as you!* *(An average 8-year old weighs 25kg.)

TRUE COLOURS

What colour is your hair?

About 90% of all people in the world have either very dark or black hair...

...while 9% have either brown or blonde hair...

...and less than 1% have red hair.

IT'S ONLY NATURAL...

About 69% of women in the UK dye their hair...

...and 17% of women have forgotten what their *natural* hair colour is!

Before the invention of modern hair dyes, people would use natural ingredients to colour their hair, including:

 Henna

Black walnut shells

Leeks

TOUGH STUFF

Your hair has superpowers...

An individual hair can hold 0.1kg in weight.

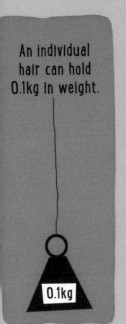

0.1kg

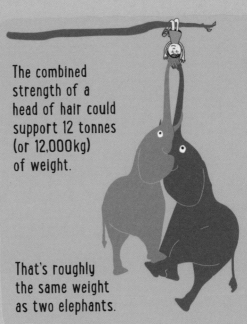

The combined strength of a head of hair could support 12 tonnes (or 12,000kg) of weight.

That's roughly the same weight as two elephants.

In 2012, a 42-year-old Chinese woman called Xu Huijun pulled two 4.5-tonne jeeps with her hair.

HAIR TODAY, GONE TOMORROW...

About 50 of your hairs fall out every day. But don't worry, they're replaced by new ones!

Hairs last for an average of four years before falling out.

2016	2017
2018	2019

FACE FUZZ

Which are the weirdest beards and the flashiest 'tashes?

Regular moustache

Pencil moustache

Handlebar moustache

Horseshoe moustache

Mutton chops

Friendly mutton chops

Goatee

Goat patch

Chin curtain

Chin strap

Soul patch

Regular beard

The longest beard ever recorded belonged to Hans Langseth. It measured 5.33m when he died (in 1927) and he left it to the Smithsonian Museum in Washington D.C., USA.

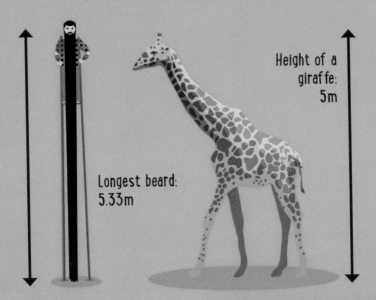

Height of a giraffe: 5m

Longest beard: 5.33m

The heaviest weight held by a beard is 63.80kg.

That's about the same weight as the average British woman.

Nobody knows why men can grow beards. Theories include:

 To keep the skin on the face warm.

 To keep the skin on the face cool, by protecting it from sunlight.

 To offer extra protection, by cushioning blows felt in a fight.

WHAT ON EARTH ARE *THOSE* CALLED?

If it's a part of your body, it's got a name...

1

The skin between your eyebrows is known as the *glabella*.

2

The red blob in the corner of your eye is your *lacrimal caruncle*.

3

The groove between the bottom of the nose and the upper lip is known as a person's *philtrum*.

4

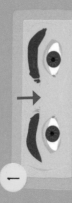

The lowest point of your chin is called the *gnathion*.

A gap between two ribs is called the *intercostal space*.

8 The creases on the undersides of your wrists are known as your *rasceta*.

10 The scientific name for your big toe is a *hallux*... (not a *Horcrux*... that's an object from *Harry Potter*).

5 An *axilla* is not a mythical monster... It's the scientific name for an armpit.

7 The white area at the bottom of your fingernail is called the *lunula*.

9 The stretchy bit of skin between your thumb and forefinger is called the *purlicue*.

WHAT ON EARTH ARE *THOSE* FOR?

There are many parts of the body that aren't particularly useful...

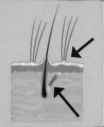

GOOSEBUMPS

Each of our hairs has a muscle that pulls it upright when we're cold or scared. This was useful when we had big, shaggy coats. But now goosebumps are just a bit creepy...

THE *PLICA SEMILUNARIS*

This is the small fold of tissue next to your *lacrimal caruncle* (see previous page). It could be the remains of a second eyelid, which humans no longer have. It may have opened and closed sideways like a reptile's!

Do they pick up radio signals..?

MEN'S NIPPLES

Since they don't ever breastfeed infants, nobody really knows why men have nipples.

WISDOM TEETH

These huge molars were useful when humans ate lots of tough meat. Now, they usually appear only in adulthood. Many people have them removed because they hurt so much!

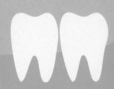

THE TONSILS
These are at the back of your throat. They help us to fight germs but we don't really need them – and many people have them taken out if they keep getting infected.

THE APPENDIX
This is a narrow tube linked to the large intestine. It helps to digest cellulose, which plants are full of. When humans ate lots of plants, this was helpful... but these days the appendix has much less to do.

THE TAILBONE (OR COCCYX)
When we all had tails, this was useful. But as humans learned to walk upright, our tails gradually got smaller – and the remaining vertebrae merged to form the small coccyx.

A BABY'S 'GRASP REFLEX'
Babies can grasp your finger REALLY hard. In fact, many can support their own weight when hanging by their own grip. Although this ability isn't necessary anymore, scientists think it might be left over from when babies used to hang on to their mother's backs. And those backs were HAIRY!!

I'm a little MONKEY!

EAR WE GO

Heard any of these facts before..?

Most people think of their ears as the sticky-out, squashy-and-blobby bits on the sides of their heads. But this is just the *PINNA*...

...most of your ear is actually INSIDE your head.

Ear canal

Eardrum

Inner ear

Eustachian tube (connects to throat)

Pinna (ear flap)

Middle ear

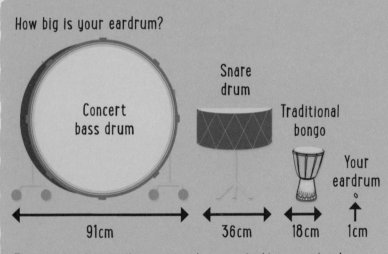

How big is your eardrum?

Concert bass drum

Snare drum

Traditional bongo

Your eardrum

91cm

36cm

18cm

1cm

Though it's a lot smaller, your eardrum works like a regular drum. It's a thin strip of skin stretched tightly across your ear canal. It vibrates when sounds hit it – just like a drum when it's struck.

STICKY STUFF

Earwax is brilliant. It cleans your ears and stops dirt and water from getting in. There are two basic types.

WET EARWAX
This is yellowy-brown and sticky – most commonly found in people with European and African ancestors.

DRY EARWAX
This is usually grey and flaky. People with Asian ancestors are more likely to have this type.

Did you know that earwax MOVES? It oozes slowly down the ear canal, taking any dirt or germs with it.

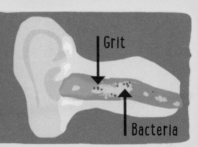

Grit

Bacteria

In 2014, US politician Joe Garcia was captured on TV while PICKING HIS EARWAX AND EATING IT during a political meeting. GROSS!

A plug of earwax was taken from a beached blue whale in 2013. It was 25cm long!

Blue whale earwax length: 25cm

Adult hand length: 19cm

HIGHS AND LOWS

Frequency is the number of times – per second, for example – that a sound wave's rise and fall is repeated. It is measured in Hertz (Hz).

LOW FREQUENCY
Examples: the sounds made by a tuba, a rumble of thunder, a frog croaking.

HIGH FREQUENCY
Examples: a bird tweeting, a baby crying, a doorbell chiming.

Some animals can hear HIGHER frequencies than us, while some can hear LOWER ones...

LOW FREQUENCY: ∿∿∿∿ HIGH FREQUENCY:

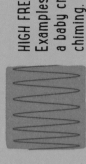

16Hz to 12,000Hz

64Hz to 23,000Hz

Children can hear much higher frequences than old people.

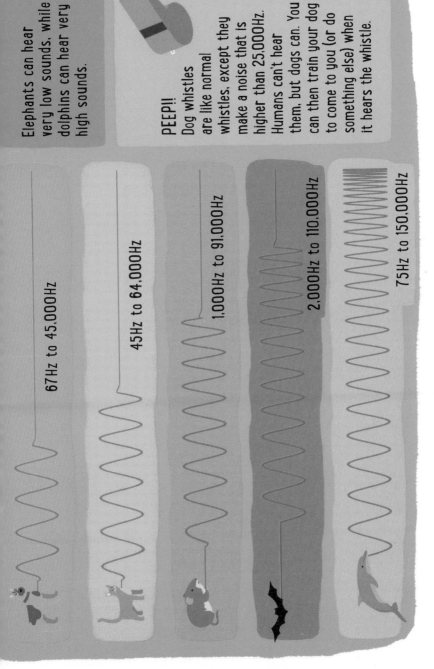

Elephants can hear very low sounds, while dolphins can hear very high sounds.

PEEP!!
Dog whistles are like normal whistles, except they make a noise that is higher than 25.000Hz. Humans can't hear them, but dogs can. You can then train your dog to come to you (or do something else) when it hears the whistle.

67Hz to 45.000Hz

45Hz to 64.000Hz

1.000Hz to 91.000Hz

2.000Hz to 110.000Hz

75Hz to 150.000Hz

TURN IT DOWN!!

Intensity is how LOUD a noise is. It is measured in decibels (dB).

DECIBELS (dB)

JET TAKING OFF: 140dB

AMBULANCE SIREN: 120dB

LAWNMOWER: 90dB

SHOUTING: 85dB

COUGHING: 80dB

Sneezing: 70dB

SNORING: 60dB

TALKING: 50dB

Innit? Yeah.

FRIDGE HUMMING: 40dB

WHISPERING: 20dB

NORMAL BREATHING: 10dB

130 — 120 — 110 — 100 — 90 — 80 — 70 — 60 — 50 — 40 — 30 — 20

OWW!!
The human pain threshold is 120dB. Anything louder will HURT. Your eardrum can burst at noise levels of 150dB or greater.

WARRPP!!
The world record for the loudest burp is held by Paul Hunn. It measured nearly 110dB...

...but the loudest snore in Britain is even more deafening. A 60-year-old granny, Jenny Chapman, snores at 111dB! Louder than a lawnmower!

TRUE OR FALSE?

YOUR EARS SHUT DOWN WHEN YOU'RE ASLEEP.

FALSE! There's no real difference in how your ears function when you're asleep. You keep on listening, your brain just chooses to 'tune out' the sounds it hears.

YOUR EARS WILL KEEP ON GROWING THROUGHOUT YOUR LIFE.

TRUE! The rest of your body stops growing at about 18 or 19 years of age. But your ears never stop. Nor does your nose! Nobody has any idea why.

SOUND TRAVELS FASTEST THROUGH THE AIR.

FALSE! Sound travels much faster through solid objects, such as walls. So, technically, we should be able to hear what our neighbours are saying! But actually – our ears have evolved to hear sounds better through the air.

YOUR EARS HELP YOU STAND UP STRAIGHT.

TRUE! Your ears contain a liquid that helps your brain to work out which way up you are. When you whizz around quickly on a roundabout, you'll often feel dizzy when you get off it. This is because the liquid in your ears has been swished around – and it takes a while for it to settle down.

SEEING THINGS

Let's have a little look at your eyes...

Your pupil lets light into your eyes. It grows or shrinks depending on how bright your surroundings are.

PUPIL   IRIS

When it's very bright or sunny, your pupil gets smaller, allowing less light into the eye.

Muscles in your iris control pupil size. In normal conditions, your pupil is about 5mm wide.

When it's dark, the pupil expands to a width of almost 9mm. This lets in 20 TIMES MORE LIGHT!

Humans have circular pupils. But what about other animals?

CATS: oval slits	SHEEP: horizontal slots	CUTTLEFISH: a 'W' shape	STINGRAY: a crescent shape	GECKO: a 'string of beads'

Cats' pupils are incredible. They start out as narrow slits, but they can grow to THREE TIMES the size of human pupils. This usually happens when it's dark or when the cat's about to pounce.

Your iris is the coloured part of your eye.
Which colour are your irises?

30% of Brits have GREEN eyes.

48% of people in Britain have BLUE eyes.

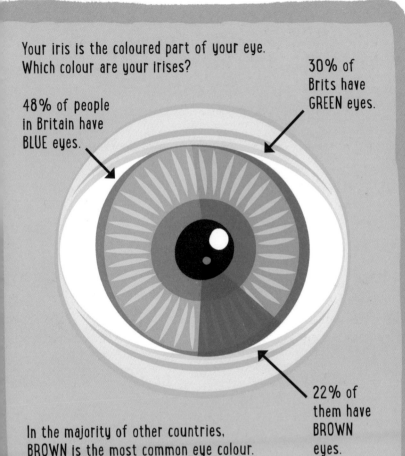

22% of them have BROWN eyes.

In the majority of other countries, BROWN is the most common eye colour.

HETEROCHROMIA
This is a condition in which the irises are a mixture of colours.
It can occur in three different forms:

1. The irises are two totally different colours.

2. A section of the iris is a different colour.

3. The irises are a different colour near to the pupil.

BLINK AND YOU'LL MISS IT

Blinking keeps your eyes clean and moist.
But some people do it more than others.

0 seconds

ADULTS when they're tired: 20 times per minute.

ADULTS
when they're
wide awake: 15
times a minute.

TEENAGERS:
ten times
a minute.

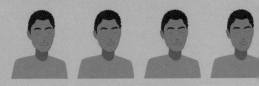

BABIES:
twice a
minute.

KIDS' STUFF
Nobody really knows why babies
don't blink very much. Some scientists
think it's because they sleep such a lot.
This means their eyes don't get as dry...

STARE OUT!
Fish and snakes don't have eyelids, so they can't blink. It's also hard to tell when they're asleep!

60 seconds

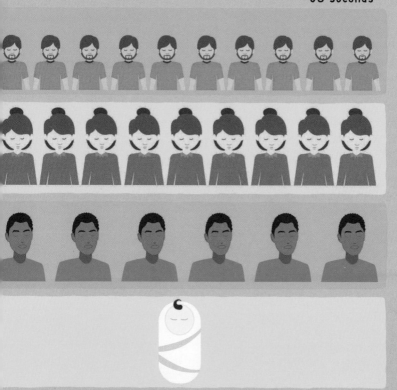

...others think it's because babies' eyes are smaller. This means they don't get as much dirt and dust in their eyes.

A SECOND LOOK...

Your eyes can play tricks on you.

How many prongs does
this fork have?

Can you see a completely red triangle here?
Because there isn't one...

...and how many legs do you think this elephant has?

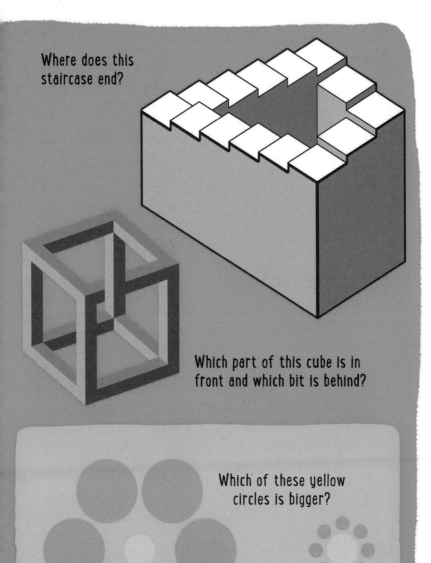

Where does this staircase end?

Which part of this cube is in front and which bit is behind?

Which of these yellow circles is bigger?

They're actually the same size. Your eyes are TERRIBLE at judging the size of circles.

DRY YOUR EYES

No need to cry about it.

Humans shed three kinds of tears:

BASAL TEARS
These keep the eye wet and protect it from bacteria.

REFLEX TEARS
If your eye becomes irritated by grit or dirt, these tears can help to flush it out.

EMOTIONAL TEARS
These are the tears you shed when you're hurt, sad or otherwise upset. Only humans cry this kind of tears.

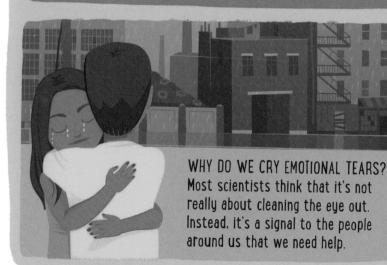

WHY DO WE CRY EMOTIONAL TEARS? Most scientists think that it's not really about cleaning the eye out. Instead, it's a signal to the people around us that we need help.

GENDER SPLIT

Women cry:

around 47 times a year

Women cry for an average of: **6 minutes**

Men cry:

around 12 times a year

Men cry for an average of: **2½ minutes**

SO... WHY DO WOMEN CRY MORE?

 Women have smaller tear ducts than men, so the liquid spills over into the eye more readily.

 Women also produce more prolactin – a hormone associated with emotion and tears.

Does crying help? Sometimes, yes. In a recent study, people were asked how they felt after weeping...

FELT BETTER: **30%**

FELT THE SAME: **60%**

FELT WORSE: **9%**

WHY DO WE SOMETIMES CRY WHEN WE LAUGH?

Nobody really knows. Some people think it's because, when we laugh, we screw up our faces and put pressure on our tear ducts. Others think it's because tears get released whenever we feel a strong emotion – and that includes being happy!

DID YOU KNOW

that tears and saliva are basically the same? They're both made up of water, proteins, salt and hormones. Your eyes are full of SPIT!

WHAT A SPECTACLE!

More than half of people in the UK are short- or long-sighted.

SHORT-SIGHTED
You can see objects clearly when they are close up, but not when they are further away.

LONG-SIGHTED
You can see things clearly when they are further away, but not when they are near.

Many people with vision problems wear glasses.
There are lots of styles to choose from!

Square
glasses

Round
glasses

Oval
glasses

Horn-rimmed
glasses

A monocle

Rimless
glasses

Dark
glasses

Half-Moon
glasses

A lorgnette

Diamond-studded
glasses

Pince-nez
glasses

Showbiz
glasses

Some people also choose to wear contact lenses!

TONNES OF TONES

You can see a rainbow...

The human eye can tell the difference between around 10 MILLION colours.

The top one is 'light brown' and the bottom one is 'dark beige'.

The back of the eye, called the retina, contains two types of 'photoreceptor' cells:

RODS
These help us to see light and dark.

CONES
These help us to see colours.

YOU HAVE...

17 times more rods than cones and approximately...

...120 MILLION rods and 7 MILLION cones.

Most of the cones are at the very centre of your retinas.

Different colours have different wavelengths.
They can be measured in nanometres (nm):

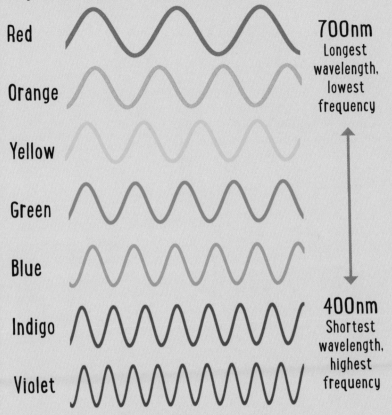

Red

Orange

Yellow

Green

Blue

Indigo

Violet

700nm
Longest
wavelength,
lowest
frequency

400nm
Shortest
wavelength,
highest
frequency

Different types of cone cells deal with these different
wavelengths, or COLOURS:

More than 50% of them deal with RED.

About 33% of them deal with GREEN.

Less than 5% deal with BLUE.

CONE CELLS don't work very well in low light levels. This is why, in a dark room, you basically see in black and white...

YOUR ROOM BY DAY

YOUR ROOM AT NIGHT

WHAT CAUSES 'AFTER-IMAGES'?

If we stare at a bright colour for too long, the cones responsible for that colour can get exhausted. Then, when your eyes look at something new, your cones are too tired to see it. So instead, your brain keeps seeing the old image... sometimes for AGES afterwards!

WHY DO WE GET 'RED EYE' IN FLASH PHOTOS?

When a camera flash goes off, sometimes the light can rush through your pupil and hit the back of your eye. Your eye then appears red because the back of your eye has a lot of BLOOD in it!

COLOUR BLINDNESS

About eight per cent of men and just under one per cent
of women in northern Europe are 'colour blind'.

Red-green colour blindness is the most common kind.
Here are some tests that help to identify the condition:

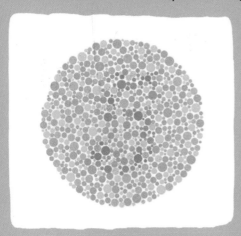

Most people can see
the number '5' in this
picture. But those
with red-green colour
blindness often see
the number '2'.

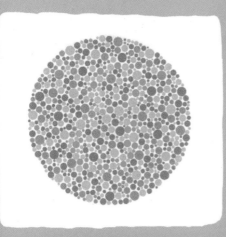

In this test, most
people see an '8'.
Those who are
red-green colour
blind usually see
the number '3'.

Blue-yellow colour blindness is a less common
condition, and there is no real test for it.

CULTURE SHOCK
Colours mean different things in different cultures

When a loved one dies, the colour of mourning is...

RED:
South Africa

WHITE:
India

BLACK:
Western Europe
and the USA

On the stock exchange...

Disaster.

Hurrah!!

21.00	21.00	34.00	26.00
42.05	42.05	45.08	32.
37.00	17.00	24.00	41.
22.05	45.05	34.11	32.
31.00	23.00	35.00	31.

21.00	21.00	34.00	2.
42.05	42.05	45.08	32.
37.00	17.00	24.00	41.
22.05	45.05	34.11	32.
31.00	23.00	35.00	31.

UK and USA:
GREEN: stocks are RISING in value.
RED: stocks are FALLING in value.

JAPAN:
GREEN: stocks are FALLING in value.
RED: stocks are RISING in value.

When drawing a picture of the Sun...

A British child
would colour
it yellow.

A Japanese
child would
colour it red.

Green for GO?

Yes, for traffic lights in most countries...

...but in Japan, sometimes BLUE means GO.

When people get married, the bride will traditionally wear...

WHITE: UK, USA and other western countries

RED: China

And cultural colours change over time, too.

A hundred years ago, boys were often dressed in pink or red and girls tended to wear blue. Now it's the other way around.

THAT'S NOT THE WAY *I* SEE IT...

Animals see colours in many different ways.

Monkeys and birds have good colour vision. They often choose their mates based on how attractively coloured they are.

A peacock's tail

A male bowerbird's colourful nest

A baboon's bottom

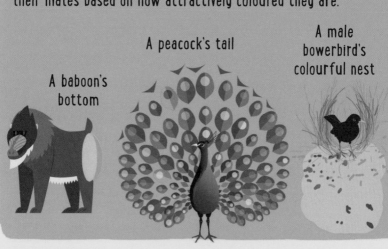

I can't STAND that shade of grey!

Bulls see the world in black and white.

In bullfighting, the bull reacts to the waving of the flag, not the flag's colour.

Dogs and cats are essentially red-green colourblind. They see most colours as yellow or blue.

What we see | What a dog sees

Some insects have *incredible* colour vision. Bees can see an *ultraviolet* spectrum of colours that are invisible to us:

What we see | What a bee sees

Rattlesnakes can detect the *infrared* parts of the spectrum:

What we see | What a rattlesnake sees

This means that, even when it's pitch black, these snakes can see a 'heat image' of their dinner...

WE ARE THE CHAMPIONS...?

Humans rule... right?

ARE WE THE FASTEST?

Nope.

Usain Bolt
(fastest human)
45km/h (28mph)

Kangaroo
48km/h (30mph)

Rabbit
56km/h (35mph)

Ostrich
64km/h (40mph)

Wildebeest
80km/h (50mph)

Cheetah
97km/h (60mph)

ARE WE THE STRONGEST?

Nah.

Heaviest weight lifted by a human (Paul Anderson):

2,844kg

9.000kg

Weight easily lifted by an African elephant:

9,000kg

A rhinoceros beetle can lift 850 times its own bodyweight. If you could do the same, you'd be able to lift two double-decker buses.

CAN WE SEE THE FURTHEST?

Afraid not.

A hawk's eyesight is about EIGHT TIMES more powerful than ours. A hawk can see a rodent scurrying around on the floor from 3 kilometres up in the sky.

CAN WE HEAR THE BEST?

No.

The greater wax moth has hearing 150 times more sensitive than ours. This helps it to hear the high-pitched chirps of its main predator — bats.

CAN WE SMELL THE BEST?

No way.

Bloodhounds have around 60 TIMES as many smell receptors as we have.

NUMBER OF SMELL RECEPTORS:

Human: 5 million

Bloodhound: around 300 million

SO WHAT *ARE* WE THE BEST AT?
Think about it...

BRAIN POWER

Among animals, the human brain is truly unique.

FOREBRAIN
The forebrain contains the cerebral cortex. The cerebral cortex handles thought, language and problem-solving. Relative to total brain size, it is bigger in humans than in any other animal.

MIDBRAIN
This area handles eye movements, hearing, movement and temperature control.

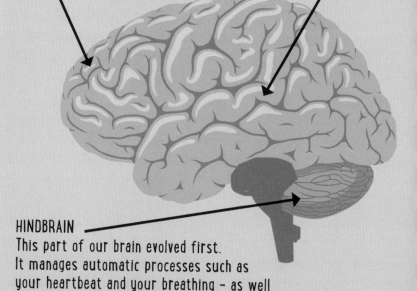

HINDBRAIN
This part of our brain evolved first. It manages automatic processes such as your heartbeat and your breathing – as well as stuff like sneezing, coughing and vomiting.

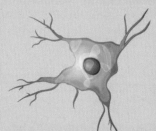

BUILT TO LAST
There are around 100 billion nerve cells in the brain. They are designed to last a lifetime. Unlike other cells, they cannot be replaced once they've died.

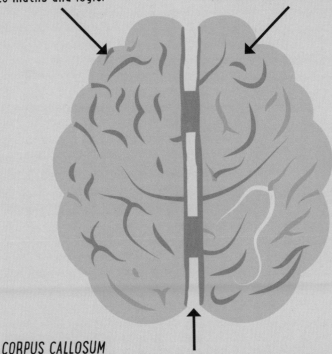

LEFT HEMISPHERE
If you are right-handed, the left-hand side of your brain is dominant. This side of the brain is often linked to maths and logic.

RIGHT HEMISPHERE
If you are left-handed, the right-hand side of your brain is dominant. This side is usually associated with emotion and creativity.

CORPUS CALLOSUM
This transmits information between the two halves of your brain. For most tasks, the two hemispheres work together.

PAINLESS
The brain has no pain sensors. If someone prodded your brain, you wouldn't feel it.

BRAIN WAVES

An electroencephalogram (EEG) is a recording of brain activity. It can be mind-blowing!

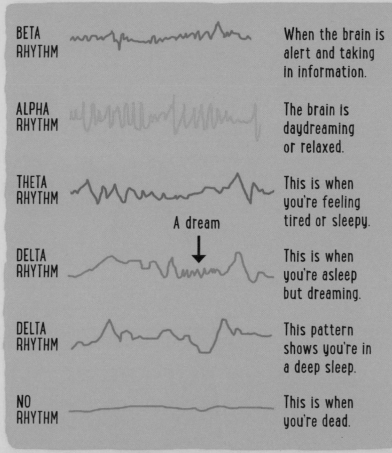

BETA RHYTHM

When the brain is alert and taking in information.

ALPHA RHYTHM

The brain is daydreaming or relaxed.

THETA RHYTHM

This is when you're feeling tired or sleepy.

A dream
↓

DELTA RHYTHM

This is when you're asleep but dreaming.

DELTA RHYTHM

This pattern shows you're in a deep sleep.

NO RHYTHM

This is when you're dead.

BRIGHT SPARKS
When you're awake, your brain activity can generate enough electricity to power a light bulb.

SWEET DREAMS

Your brain is often more active when you're asleep.
But what do different dreams mean?

BEING CHASED
This is one of the most common dreams. It usually means there is something in your life that you're trying to avoid. Time to face it!

FLYING
This represents how much control we have over our lives. If you're flying high, you're in control. If you can't quite take off, then someone or something is holding you back.

DOING AN EXAM
This usually means you're being tested in your life. Often your dream is trying to show you that you can learn from something in your past.

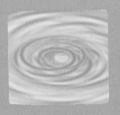

WATER
Water is meant to represent our emotions. If the water in your dream is choppy or swirling, then you're feeling upset.

FALLING
Falling dreams usually mean you're feeling overwhelmed. Ask for some help!

BRAIN TEASERS

How good are you at thinking *sideways*?

1

You are in a dark room with a candle, a small stove and a gas lamp. You only have ONE match, so what do you light first?

2

The day before yesterday, Barry was seven years old. Next year, he'll be ten. How is this possible?

3

A cowboy was going to Dallas on his horse. It took him two days to get there, he stayed there for one day and it took him one day to get back. He went on Tuesday and came back on Tuesday! But how?

4

If you are running a race, which place are you in if you overtake the person who is in second place?

5

How much dirt is there in a hole that is one metre wide and one metre deep?

6

A family of four and their pet dog were crowded under a very small umbrella – but none of them got wet. Why was that?

7

There are only two barbers in town. One has nice, tidy hair and one has messy hair. To which barber should you go to get your hair cut?

Answers

1. The match!
2. Barry was born on December 31st. It is now January 1st. He was seven on December 30th (the day before yesterday), and he turned eight on December 31st. So, THIS year he will turn nine (on December 31st) and NEXT year he will have his tenth birthday.
3. *Tuesday* was the name of his horse.
4. Second! There's still someone running in front of you.
5. There's no dirt in a hole!
6. It wasn't raining.
7. Try the messy-haired one! Because there are only two barbers, they probably cut each other's hair. That would mean the barber with the messy hair cuts the hair of the neat-haired barber.

TALK TALK

These facts about language will leave you speechless.

How many words can humans speak at different ages?

NEWBORN

No words

12 MONTHS

1 word

18 MONTHS

20 words

2 YEARS

200 words

3 YEARS

1,000 words

8 YEARS

10,000 words

MOST COMMON FIRST WORDS

mummy

daddy

dog

duck

cat

teddy

more

milk

baby

ball

THE SPOKEN WORD

The letters 'ough' can be pronounced at least eight different ways:

rough (*uff*)
dough (*oh*)
thought (*aw*)
plough (*ow*)
through (*oo*)
cough (*off*)
thorough (*er*)
hiccough (*up*)

NEW WORDS

The dictionary grows by about 4,000 words a year. Recent new entries include:

SD card

tomoz

air punch

selfie

cool beans

WINNING WORDS

QUEUEING is the only word with five vowel letters in a row.

RHYTHMS is the longest English word containing no vowels.

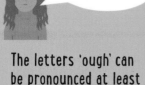

SCREECHED is the longest one-syllable word in English.

ANGRY and *HUNGRY* are the only two words in English that end with the letters 'gry'.

BLOWING HOT AND COLD

What happens when your body temperature changes?

TOO HOT

45°C Dead

41°C You pass out. Brain damage is likely.

40°C A bad fever. You start seeing things that aren't really there!

38°C Things start getting sweaty...

37°C A normal body temperature. All's good.

BRRRRR!!!

CHATTER-CHATTER
Chattering teeth are just a type of shivering. Your face muscles are trying to warm up by quivering, so your teeth get shaken up.

COOL IT!
Sweating helps to cool us down. The average person produces ONE LITRE of sweat per day. In three months, you could fill a bath with your sweat!

34°C Shivers, chattering teeth and goosebumps. You'll probably feel like weeing.

32°C A really bad fit of the shivers, and shallow breathing.

31°C Your blood rushes to your vital organs to keep them warm.

30°C You'll start seeing and hearing things.

29°C Even though you're cold, your skin feels like it's on fire!

25°C Dead

TOO COLD

Lovely weather!

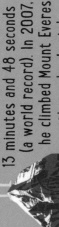

THE ICEMAN
In 2008, Wim Hof sat in a bath of ice for one hour, 13 minutes and 48 seconds (a world record). In 2007, he climbed Mount Everest wearing only shorts!

IN COLD BLOOD
Cold-blooded animals don't have a regular or 'standard' body temperature. It changes all the time.

For example, if it's 20°C outside, then a snake's body temperature will drop to 20°C. If it's 30°C outside, the snake will slowly warm up and reach 30°C too.

HEART OF THE MATTER

Your heart pumps blood around your body. This is how.

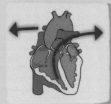

Blood is first pumped from the right-hand side of your heart and through your lungs – to pick up OXYGEN.

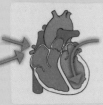

The blood returns to the left-hand side of your heart, carrying oxygen. In other words, the blood is now 'oxygenated'.

The left-hand side of your heart then pumps the oxygenated blood all around your body.

Blood travels away from the heart through your ARTERIES.

Once it has reached all of your body's tissues and organs, blood returns to your heart through the VEINS.

Then it starts all over again.

EYE KNOW

Blood carries oxygen around the body. It is needed for energy and growth.

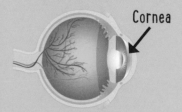

Cornea

The only part of your body that has no blood supply is the cornea – the clear layer on the outside of your eye. It gets its oxygen directly from the air.

THUMPETY-THUMP

There are valves in your heart to make sure the blood only flows one way. Can you feel your heart beating?

This is the sound that these valves make as they open and close.

LONG JUMP

The heart pumps blood at very high pressure. It can squirt blood about NINE METRES out of your body.

Longest ever long jump: Mike Powell, 8.95m

Blood squirted from body: 9m

A BIT OF A STRETCH

If you stretched out all the blood vessels in your body, they would be nearly 100,000km long. That's enough to circle the globe more than TWICE.

BEAT IT

Sometimes, your heart has to work *hard*...

YOUR HEARTBEAT – measured in bpm (beats per minute):

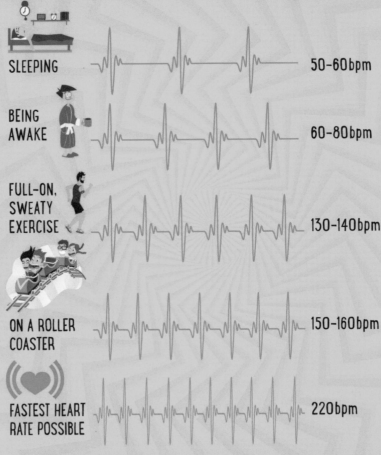

SLEEPING — 50–60bpm

BEING AWAKE — 60–80bpm

FULL-ON, SWEATY EXERCISE — 130–140bpm

ON A ROLLER COASTER — 150–160bpm

FASTEST HEART RATE POSSIBLE — 220bpm

BABY BOOM
A newborn baby has a much higher heart rate, usually around 150bpm. It is burning food fast and growing fast, which means its heart needs to work harder to deliver oxygen around its body.

PUMP IT UP

How much blood does your heart pump through your body?

IN A MINUTE: 5 LITRES

IN AN HOUR: 300 LITRES
(that's four baths full!)

IN A DAY: 7,200 LITRES
(that's a skip full!)

IN A YEAR: 2.63 MILLION LITRES
(that could fill an Olympic-sized swimming pool!)

NOTE: these are all average figures. The exact amounts depend on your age and size.

WILD AT HEART

How do other animals' hearts compare to ours?

BIG BEATS

The blue whale has the most incredible heart in the animal kingdom.

Its heart is BIGGER than any other animal's:

0.6 tonnes

That's about the same weight as a car.

It has the SLOWEST heart rate...

THREE BEATS per minute (when diving)

SIX BEATS per minute (when surfacing)

...a wood frog's heart goes even slower, but only when it hibernates. In winter, its heart STOPS and ice crystals form in its blood. It starts to beat again when the weather gets warmer.

The whale's heart PUMPS:

7,000 litres

of blood around its body. A human heart pumps about five litres.

Its major arteries are so WIDE that a child could crawl through them:

Blue whale aorta (diameter): 25cm

Football (diameter): 22cm

TALL STORY

The giraffe has one of the STRONGEST hearts. Its blood pressure is twice as high as ours. That's because it has to get the blood up to the top of its 1.8-metre neck, fighting gravity all along the way!

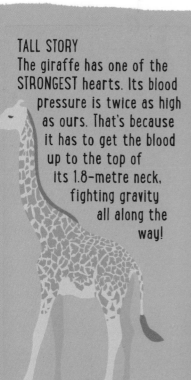

THE MOST HEARTS

How MANY hearts do animals have?

♥ Most living creatures (including humans)

♥♥♥ Octopuses and squids

♥♥♥♥ Hagfish

♥♥♥♥♥ Worms

Worm hearts are arranged side by side – near their heads. They are very simple hearts and don't have the valves and chambers that human hearts have.

HEARTLESS BEASTS

Many animals have NO HEARTS at all:

STARFISH

SPONGES

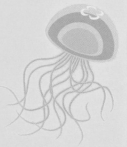

JELLYFISH

These animals also have no bones... and no brains!

FOLLOW YOUR NOSE

Your nose has lots of important jobs to do.

 It SMELLS things. Humans can detect *more than a trillion* different smells.

 It helps you to BREATHE.

 It helps you to TASTE food. When you have a blocked nose, it's hard to taste anything.

It PRODUCES SNOT and mucus (about a litre a day) to protect you from bacteria.

 It helps you to REMEMBER things. Smells can trigger memories from many years ago.

 It WARMS UP AIR before it reaches your lungs – very handy on cold days.

 It grows if you TELL LIES (...no, sorry, that was just *Pinocchio*).

 It allows you to SNEEZE (*see the next page*). Sneezes travel at about 63km/h (39mph).

BLESS YOU!!

Not everybody sneezes the same way...

SILENT SNEEZERS
Some people try to hold it in. They let out a little noise – *"Uh-fnff"* – and they screw up their faces as if they've just smelt something stinky.

TRUMPETERS
These people are the opposite. They make AS MUCH NOISE AS POSSIBLE. Spit and snot flies everywhere.

BIG-BAD-WOLF SNEEZERS
These people huff and puff before they LET RIP. "Ah... aah... *AAAHHH...*" and then they *blow the house down.*

MULTIPLE SNEEZERS
Some people fire off a few in a row. Usually, they'll give off a little "Oh dear" at the end.

SHOULDER SNEEZERS
These people turn their heads to one side and sneeze onto their shoulder. Nobody knows why.

TRADITIONAL SNEEZERS
These people are the most polite. They sneeze at a normal volume and hold a tissue or their hand over their mouth and nose.

Scientists say your style of sneeze is genetic – in other words, you inherited it from your mother or father... so blame THEM!

ROTTEN STINKERS

Here's our round-up of the SMELLIEST things on the planet.

THE STINK BUG
Stink bugs release a spray from their abdomens to prevent them from being eaten by birds and lizards. In America, they often invade people's houses and are almost impossible to get rid of.

Stinky rating:

VIEUX BOULOGNE CHEESE
This is the smelliest cheese in the whole wide world. Its stink has been compared to rotting leaves and cowpats. It can be smelt from about 50 metres away.

Stinky rating:

THE STINKBIRD
The hoatzin or stinkbird smells like manure. This is because it breaks down its food in its throat (or 'foregut'), rather than in its stomach. No other bird does this.

Stinky rating:

DURIAN

This Asian fruit smells like poo and rotten onions. In Singapore, signs on trains say 'NO DURIANS' – because they can stink out an entire carriage. However, many people enjoy the taste of them.

Stinky rating:

THE SKUNK

If a skunk doesn't like you, it'll will cover you with its stink spray. It can hit you from about three metres away. It's very hard to remove the smell from clothes... some experts say you're better off throwing the clothes away!

Stinky rating:

THE BOMBARDIER BEETLE

When disturbed, this insect sprays a stinky chemical in all directions. It shoots out so fast it makes a "popping" noise. The spray is also BOILING HOT. If it hits your skin, it's both smelly AND painful!

Stinky rating:

THE CORPSE PLANT

This is a three-metre-wide orchid that smells like a dead body. Even if it's half a kilometre away, you'll still be able to detect its stench.

Stinky rating:

TAKE A DEEP BREATH...

How long can YOU hold your breath for?

An average person:

30 seconds

Average person in excellent health:

2 minutes

Japanese pearl diver:

7 minutes

Among mammals, the Cuvier's beaked whale is the breath-holding champion. It can dive without taking a breath for more than TWO-AND-A-QUARTER hours.

DIVE! DIVE!! DIVE!!!
Humans can hold their breath for much longer underwater than they can on land. This is because of a 'diving reflex' that slows down our heart rate.

David Blaine, magician:

17 minutes and 4 seconds

Tom Sietas, 'freediver' and world record holder:

22 minutes and 22 seconds

SPLUTTER!

GURGLE!!

Southern elephant seals can stay underwater for about TWO HOURS without breathing.

Green sea turtles are even more incredible. These reptiles can stay underwater for FIVE HOURS without coming up for air.

LIFE BEGINS AT 80

As we grow old, our bodies don't work quite as well.
But does that mean life is over...? NO!!

Fauja Singh completed a
26-mile marathon in Toronto,
Canada, aged 100. Harriet
Thompson, aged 92, did the
same in San Diego, USA.

At the age of 76, Russian grandmother Sakinat
Khanapiyeva performed several impressive feats
of strength – such as lifting a 24-kg dumbbell
and snapping iron horseshoes.

At the age of 86, Johanna Quaas of
Germany was still regularly competing
in gymnastics exhibitions.

When he was 73, a South African named Otto Thaning swam
the English Channel. This is a non-stop, 21-mile journey – and
the strong currents often add to the distance.

At 80 years of age, a Japanese climber called Yuichiro Miura made it to the top of Mount Everest.

Dorothy Custer celebrated her 102nd birthday by base jumping from the Perrine Bridge in Idaho, USA.

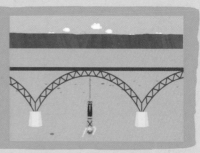

Forrest Lunsway and Rose Pollard got married when he was 100 and she was 90 years old.

At 77, former American astronaut John Glenn went back into orbit on board the space shuttle *Discovery*. The shuttle orbited Earth 134 times.

HOUSEHOLD GERMS

Where in your house will you find the most bacteria per square centimetre (cm²)..?

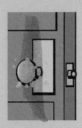

DOORKNOB:
1,240 bacteria per cm²

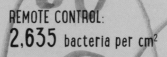

REMOTE CONTROL:
2,635 bacteria per cm²

KEYBOARD MOUSE:
12,400 bacteria per cm²

KITCHEN TAP:
35,650 bacteria per cm²

DISH SPONGE:
120,000,000 bacteria per cm²

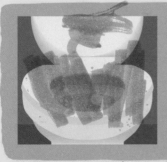

Surprisingly, toilet seats have only around 186 bacteria per square centimetre. People tend to disinfect their toilet frequently, so it's often the cleanest place in the house!

THIS IS THE END

Ever seen a zombie? Well, guess what? You're SURROUNDED by them. People are covered with DEAD STUFF.

The hairs on your body are DEAD. They have no blood supply and they can't feel pain. They're made of keratin – a tough, long-lasting protein.

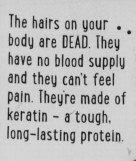

The outer layers of your skin are composed of DEAD cells. They protect the living cells below them.

The visible parts of your teeth are also DEAD. They are made of enamel and have no DNA nor any cellular matter. The living part of your tooth lies underneath.

Your fingernails and toenails are made up of DEAD cells. Like your hair, they consist of keratin.

SOURCES

This book would not have been possible without a wide range of other books, not to mention magazines, websites, tweets and TV shows. Here are some of the best.

BRILLIANT BOOKS:
Guinness World Records (Guinness World Records, 2014)
Ripley's Believe It Or Not 2014 by Ripley Publishing (Random House, 2013)
The Knowledge Encyclopedia (Dorling Kindserley, 2013)
SuperHuman Encyclopedia (Dorling Kindersley, 2014)
The Ultimate Book About ME by Richard Platt (Carlton Books/Science Museum, 2014)
5,000 Awesome Facts (About Everything) (National Geographic, 2012)
That's Gross! (National Geographic, 2012)
The 'How It Works' Book of Junior Science (Imagine Publishing, 2013)
1,227 QI Facts to Blow Your Socks Off – Kindle Edition by John Lloyd and John Mitchinson (Faber and Faber, 2012).
1,339 QI Facts to Make Your Jaw Drop – Kindle Edition by John Lloyd and John Mitchinson (Faber and Faber, 2013)
The Incredible Science of You by Nick Arnold (Scholastic, 2009)
Why Is Snot Green? by Glenn Murphy (Macmillan Children's Books/Science Museum, 2007)
How Loud Can You Burp? by Glenn Murphy (Macmillan Children's Books/Science Museum, 2008)
Operation Ouch: Your Brilliant Body (Little, Brown/CBBC, 2013)
The 'How It Works' Book of Amazing Answers to Curious Questions – Kindle Edition (Imagine Publishing, 2013)

PLUS... the 'QI' TV show and the 'QI Elves' on Twitter
AND... The *Horrible Science* books (published by Scholastic) – especially *Painful Poison, Really Rotten Experiments* and *Bulging Brains*

WONDERFUL WEBSITES:
www.britannica.com • http://kids.britannica.com • http://uber-facts.com
www.guinnessworldrecords.com • www.nationalgeographic.com
http://qi.com • www.newscientist.com • www.nasa.gov
www.lookandlearn.com • www.technologyreview.com

SUPER NEWS WEBSITES:
www.bbc.co.uk/news • http://edition.cnn.com

Newspaper websites to look up:
The Guardian, The Independent, The Huffington Post, The Telegraph, and *The Daily Mail.*

And, of course, there's always the AWESOME power of 'Google'.

For a full list of all sources and references used, visit: http://goo.gL/PZGoI7